# Using Graphics In Books

# Using Graphics In Books

Raster PSD Background

All vector type

## David Bergsland

SPIRIT-FILLED FICTION AWARD OF EXCELLENCE

REALITY CALLING: CHRISTIAN SPECULATIVE FICTION

**Radiqx** PRESS

**Spirit-filled Fiction**

The Proverbial War
Guy Stanton III

All vector PDF

**Radiqx** PRESS

Written and published in August, 2016
© David Bergsland • All Rights Reserved

ISBN-13: 978-1537373805

ISBN-10: 1537373803

Produced by Radiqx Press
314 Van Brunt Street
Mankato, Minnesota 56001
http://radiqx.com • info@radiqx.com

Please let me know if there is anyway I can help you in your publishing endeavors.

*This is dedicated to all my friends and followers online who have been such an inspiration to me over the past decade*

# Contents

.

# Chapter 1

# What's the purpose of this book?

As I wander around the social media world, I regularly sense a deep confusion, and/or ignorance, about what is required in a graphic being published. So, I think it would be helpful to share some of the basics which apply to all self-publishing workflows.

- **What are the differences between vector and raster graphics:** Photoshop or Illustrator/InDesign; Gimp or Inkscape; PDF/EPS or PSD, TIFF, GIF, JPEG, PNG?

- **What are the graphic requirements for print books:** Greyscale or color?

- **What are the graphic requirements for ePUBs and MOBI books:** Fixed layout and Reflowable?

- **What are the advantages of each format:** .ai, .psd, .tif, .pdf, .eps; .gif, .jpg, .png?

- **How does this vary with the different suppliers:** Lightning Source, Createspace, Lulu, Kindle, iBooks, Kobo, and the others?

## This is not about producing images

I am not going to get into software training for Photoshop, GIMP, Illustrator, or my favorite, InDesign. I'm not even going to cover the favorite graphic software in the US—PowerPoint (I know, that's a very emotional statement for many of us. Sorry). There are too many possibilities in that direction.

My goal is to give you straight forward information about what is possible in the various file formats. I also want to share what the self-publishing suppliers require as of the Summer of 2016. As you know, that is a constantly changing target.

## Let's begin with a discussion of vector graphics

Most self publishers do not know what they are and why they are so important.

# Chapter 2

# Vector versus Raster

## Outlines or Pixels?

This is the basic division in graphics. It is critical you understand the differences—and the benefits to each graphic type. Most self-publishers assume that all graphics have pixels. This is not true. This is a very good thing.

### For example, the chapter head graphic above

It is mostly vector. In other words, it is all produced with outlines {PostScript paths, in this case]. Well, almost all, except for what?

That little soap bubble, of ink-toned water which collapsed on a sheet of paper, was then scanned, cleaned up in Photoshop, saved as a PSD and dropped above the number. Outside of the bubble, everything was drawn with vectors—specifically the PostScript paths produced with Illustrator or InDesign. The lizard, for example, was drawn and placed on top of two concentric circles with varying gradient fills for both the fill and the stroke.

So, why did I do that? Just to shake up some of your preconceptions. If you have only used PowerPoint,

Gimp, or Photoshop to produce your graphics and covers, you may have no idea what I am talking about.

I do not expect you to forget about the bit-mapped extravaganzas commonly developed in Photoshop. However, developing excellent type illustrations in InDesign and then rasterizing them in Photoshop will give you much better typographic control of your graphics. I talk about this process in my book production manual. For now, we need to understand vectors.

Scan of an old B&W greyscale ink painting

A vector conversion of the same image

Vector drawing is one of the most misunder-stood tools in our arsenal. Digital drawing, some-times known as PostScript illustration, is one of the indispensable tools of digital publishing. However, it has been lost in the hype of smart phones and digital cameras. Back in the bad ol'days (before computers), when we >gasp< had to do everything by hand, things were clearer. There was camerawork, inkwork, typesetting, and pasteup. These areas have been replaced by image manipulation, digital drawing, word processing, and page layout software. Camerawork and image manipulation are the main purpose of Photoshop & Gimp.

## Let's start with an actual graphic

It is obvious that vector drawing is very different from a painting, photograph, or any other scanned object. It's not to say that one is better than the other—they are simply different. The painting is soft, subtle, more "realistic." The vector drawing is clean, crisp, easily resizable, with a much smaller file size.

With vector graphics, we are now talking about inkwork instead of camerawork—digital drawing instead of image manipulation. What does that mean? It means that we are looking at an entirely different type of artwork. This artwork is not focused on soft transitions and subtle effects [though these are possible]. The purpose of this type of art is fundamentally different. These are images that are crisp, precise, and direct. This is where we leave the natural world and enter an environment with no dirt, no scratches, no broken parts, no garbage.

**It is also extremely easy to add professional-quality, easily resizable type to a vector drawing:** Any type added to an original painting must be drawn by hand. Even if you are working with a scan of the art in Photoshop, type is limited to large point sizes and fuzzy edges. Photoshop type needs 1200 dpi to 2400 dpi to be sharp enough for printing.

The vector landscape from the previous page can be easily resized and have type added to it. There is no fuzziness or pixelation. The type is crisp and sharp, even if it were printed out at 500% or 2500% of the original size of the drawing. If this were a Photoshop file, it would be pixelated here. By pixelated, we mean that you could see the jagged edges of the individual picture elements or pixels.

Finally, the Photoshop type would be very

crude at 200 to 300 dots per inch, whereas the vector graphic has type at the typographic standard—1,200 dpi to 2,400 dpi (or whatever the resolution of the printer is). Imagine if we printed it out at two foot wide or more. The vector image would still be sharp.

Below, we see the vector version enlarged 600%. You can see some of the drawing deficiencies, but the image is still crisp. The same would be true if we enlarged it to hang as a billboard on the side of a skyscraper at 50 yards wide. There would be no pixelization.

**However, that sharpness is not true of scanned, or bitmap, images:** The Photoshop (bitmapped) version is ruined at two feet wide, as you can see above. When the image was enlarged to two feet wide, the pixels could not change shape. So, we now see what that bitmap really looked like.

The only reason it looked smooth originally was that the pixels were a three hundredth of an inch each and that is far too small to be seen by a naked eye. In the enlargement, the pixels are about a twelfth of an inch square and easily visible. Also, this enlarged bitmapped image was 235 MB. Full page high resolution full color images like you use on your covers are often 25 MB or more. If you use many of these images in a book like this one, the file size gets huge.

The vector image remains 49 KB no matter what size you use for output. Yes, that is 235 million bytes as compared to 49 thousand bytes of data. Obviously, there are some real advantages to vector illustration.

## The two major advantages to vector art:

- **It is completely resizable**: Vector art is what is commonly referred to as *resolution independent*. There is no resolution to a vector file. All of the shapes, and this includes all the type, are defined by mathematical outlines that can be enlarged or reduced at will. The resolution is produced by the printer, screen, or Photoshop.

- **The file size is normally much smaller**: This is not always the case with very complicated vector images. However, the 49K versus 235MB comparison just mentioned is very common.

  This means that I can make my original artwork for the print version of the book and then easily resize, recolor, and convert it into any file type, size, and resolution needed for the rest of the versions.

  I can open it in Photoshop and convert it to 72 dpi (rasterize it) at the size needed for the JPEGs, GIFs, and PNGs needed for Kindle or ePUBs. I can enlarge the image to a poster or book cover and/or reduce the size to a dingbat used for bulleted lists all from the same original. This cannot be done with a bitmapped image.

**InDesign produces excellent vector images**: I cover some techniques in my book production manual. Your concern, at this point, is to make sure all of the images you use are of professional quality. You cannot use Web images for print.

The lizard is an old FreeHand drawing. I used the original from 1996 in the print versions. But I gave up on fixing it in Illustrator and colorized it in InDesign for the ebooks. It was simply too difficult to work on it within Illustrator.

## Programs which make vector images

There really are not too many: Illustrator, InDesign, FreeHand, and Corel Draw. There is a freebie named Ink- scape, but it has quite a way to go for usefulness. Of these, the dominant ones are Illustrator and InDesign. Almost all the vector cli- part and stock art you can purchase are Illus- trator files in .ai or .eps format.

Why are the lizards on this page? They show that vector images can be resized at will—from 13% above to 494% below, yet they remain sharp.

# Words, the fastest & most common graphic

Speed is one of the reasons to use words as graphics. However, this does not touch on the real reason. To cover that reason, remember that old Chinese saying, "A picture is worth a thousand words." There is truly a major problem with that old proverb. A picture does indeed speak volumes. The problem is found in controlling (or even predicting) what the image talks about with its content and implications.

Now, back to the point. I am not saying that an accurately focused, impeccably crafted illustration is not a wonder—and extremely effective. The problems are the normal ones: time and money. Excellent illustrations are very rare and expensive—if you can even locate one.

Kawasaki in *APE* talks about the need to sell 2500 books to make a profit with base costs of several thousand dollars. That's all very nice, but I don't have anywhere near that kind of budget and my niches are normally too small to support that many sales. I need graphics I can do for free [or close to it]. In addition, they must be professional to avoid the need to lower prices because of low quality. The result of all of this is that graphic treatments of words will regularly be the solution of choice, and often the best choice.

The frequency of this choice is increased by the simple fact that often there is no real graphic conceivable to describe what you really need to help sell that point about selling product, the need for faith, or that support book for your seminars offering help with depression. Words are clear, concise, and can be graphically strong.

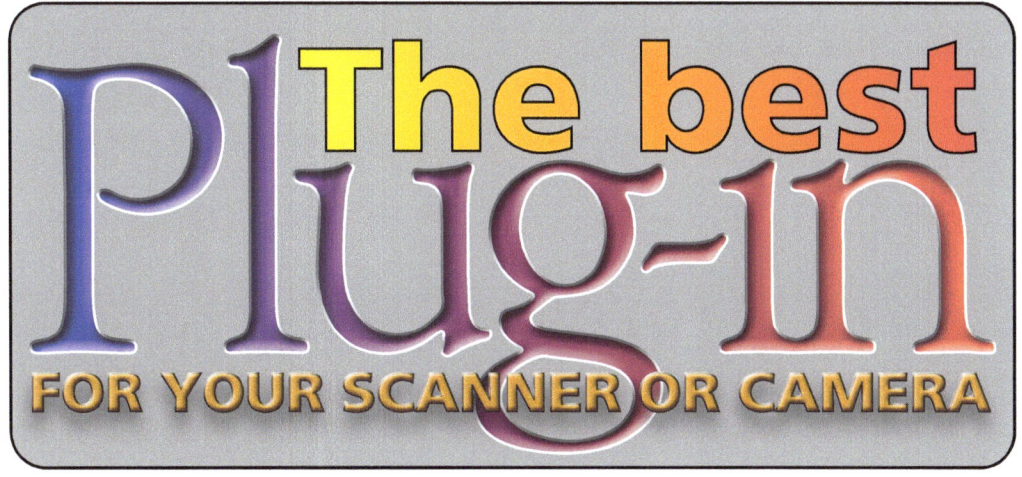

When you really need it, and can say it accurately, what works better than **FREE**? How about a snappy graphic saying whatever you need? The plug-in graphic above would not make a good headline or logo; it's not strong enough. But it certainly adds interest as a sub-head on a page where some sort of graphic is visually necessary. It could be used as a subhead or an added illustration—even a drop cap graphic. My question is: did you notice the missing dot over the i in Plug-in?

In general, you will find many occasions when a quick graphic made of words will solve your graphic dilemma handily. Often you don't even have to write those words—they are offered as part of the story you are writing. So, what we want to do in this little booklet is give you the concepts. What we need to do is give you conceptual control of what you have been doing. The actual production techniques are in other books.

## What's the point?

Vector graphics are marvelous. If you are working with all type, you can always save it as a PDF which will be all vectors. However, do not do any drawing in Word or Powerpoint. Those programs use low resolution raster images for anything except type. The pros use InDesign because nothing does type like InDesign—not even Illustrator. CorelDraw is a possible alternative, but it's quite rare and often causes production problems.

# Adding graphics to your book

Here we have a word processor problem. Graphics in Word are not usable professionally. In fact, in many cases Word cannot even add professional graphics to a Word document. Print graphics need to be vector (PDFs, EPSs, or AI files) or raster (Photoshop files, photographs, and the like). Bitmap files [raster] must be 300 dpi. More than that, photos must be sharp, in focus, with good contrast. They should be CMYK (the color space of print). This is the largest problem with GIMP, for example. It's only RGB. Even though some on-demand printers now use RGB images, the colors will change when they are converted to CMYK for printing unless you are very experienced with color. Word can handle almost none of this.

But for most of your printing, your graphics will be high resolution grayscale—so you will need to store high resolution color versions for conversions to use in your ebooks. The print version of a book normally requires greyscale images. This makes many of the demonstrations hard to see. That is why

I expect most of you will be using the ebooks: the downloadable PDFs or the fixed layout Kindle textbook and ePUB FXL in iBooks. We will talk about this in much greater depth later in the book. But I must mention a few things here.

One of the most obvious areas of amateurism is found in the images many self publishers use to promote and market their books. Even worse are some of the graphics I have seen used inside of these ebooks. Many of them are so blurry they cannot be read. Even if they are not blurry, they are commonly quite ugly and of poor quality.

## You must use professional grade images

Traditionally, an excellent professional photo cost around $300 for a single use. The truly superb images still cost that much. But in most cases, those prices are long gone. Many of the stock photo websites will sell you an image for $25 or less (commonly just a few dollars now). In addition, there are excellent sources of free images. But, you must be careful to get images for which you have a legal license.

Many of these stock photo companies also offer professional quality vector graphics also. Vector graphics are what you will need for those maps in the front of your novels, for example. Otherwise, editing the map will be exceedingly difficult. Blurry unreadable maps are the most common serious formatting flaw in reflowable ePUBs and MOBIs, and good maps are essential in genre which include world-building fiction.

## Using photos (the most common graphics used)

The best solution here is to use photos you have shot with a good digital camera. Images from your smart phone may not do. The problem is that printing quality requires 300 dpi. The latest smart phones come close to that—as long as you don't do much cropping of the images. For example, images in this book are usually five inches wide or more. That means I must have images which are 1500 pixels wide or better—after cropping. I usually get red flags on the print editions of my books when I submit them to the printing company because I use a lot of 72 dpi screen captures. In some cases, I've had to sign a release stating that I'll pay for the printed results regardless of how bad these screen captures print.

You can also use royalty-free images from the Web that give you free rights to publish as you wish. There are many sources for images like these. Wikimedia Commons is good—as are MorgueFile and Pixabay. Sites like Fotolia offer professional quality images at very reasonable prices. Just make sure you read the rights copy carefully. Many images have some restrictions, even if it is only adding a Photo Credit line next to your image. Just make sure they are large enough in pixel dimensions and in color.

**JPEGs:** You need to be very careful with JPEGs. The method of compression uses averages where you are not only lossy (image data is deleted), but they also produce bad artifacts around all the contrasty edges of the image. These can actually destroy the image beyond usability.

**Below you can see an example of extreme JPEG compression:**

The images above are more than three times the resolution of those below. At this resolution, a lot of the damage looks very small. However, at 72 dpi the image below is completely unusable except as a bad example—for print. However, 72 dpi is what is used in ePUBs and Kindle books. In color they work better. Plus a Retina Display can work wonders. Maybe they both look equally bad in an ereader, but in print they're horrible and the JPEG is much worse.

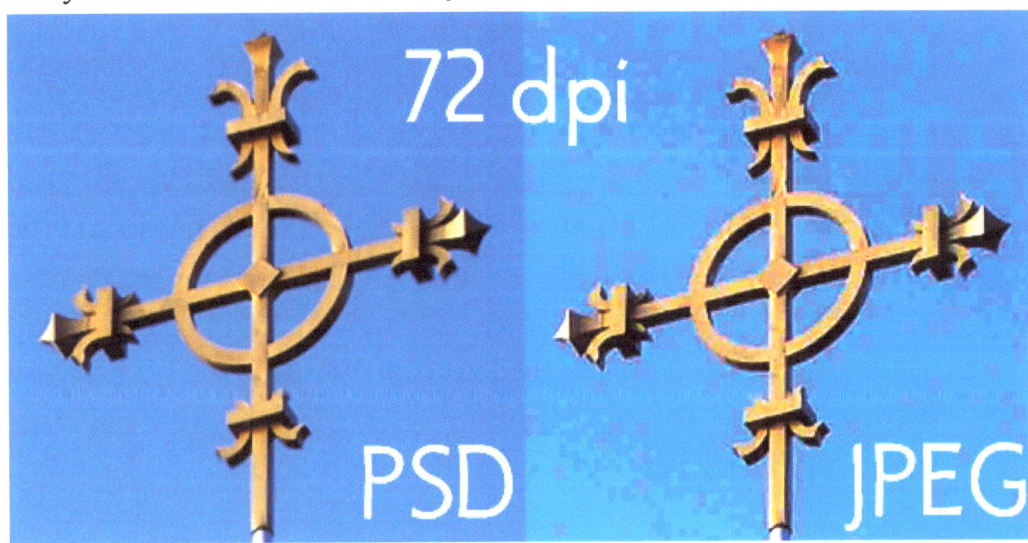

## Resaving JPEGs makes it worse

Every time you resave a JPEG at a different size or resolution you increase the damage—adding artifacts in top of artifacts. This is one of the main reason why I continually suggest that you have two sub-folders in your book folder: Originals and Links. That way you always have a clean original with no artifacts when you make edits to your images. That way your JPEGs will always be the highest quality possible.

## Using Photoshop's Save For Web command

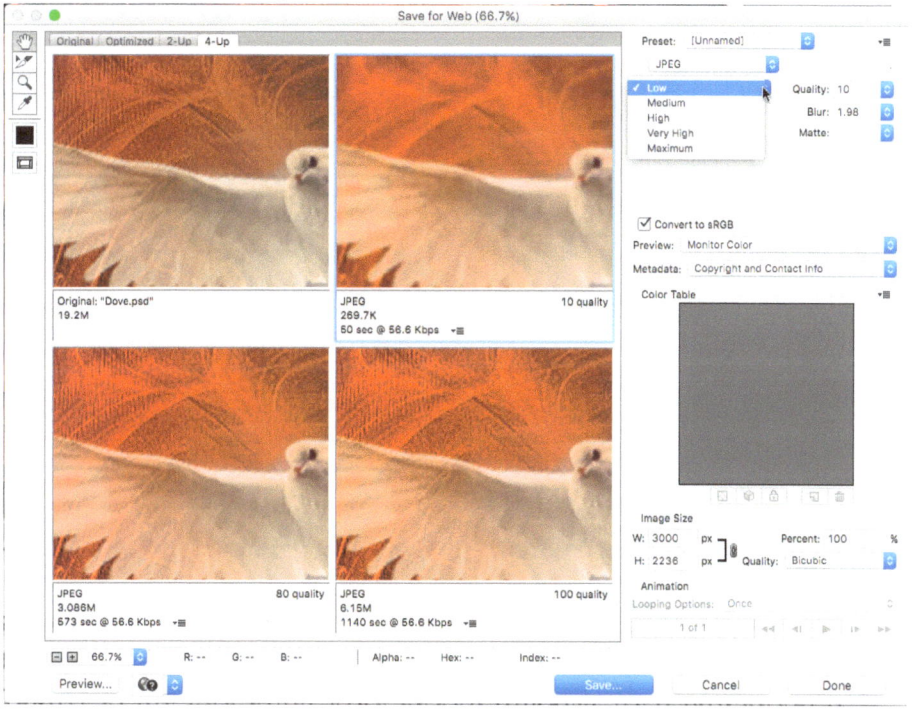

The other method for making the highest possible JPEG quality is using Photoshop's Save For Web Dialog. As you can see above, maintaining details is crucial as we are forced to lower our resolutions further and further as we go from print to reflowable ebook.

Even here, at close to print quality [over 200 dpi], you can see that detail is very hard to read. In print and PDFs, I can keep my resolution up to as close to 300 dots per inch as possible. That helps a lot. In the capture above, you can easily see how much the image has changed from the original at the top left to the other three JPEG compressions.

**Notice the file size changes:** In the original, the file size is 19.2 MB. In the maximum quality [100%] JPEG, lower right, this file size has changed to 6.15 MB. The lower left option is high quality [80%] and the file size has dropped to 3.086 MB. However, the low quality [10%] plus the 1.98 blur version on the top right has a file size of 269.7 KB—yes, kilobytes not megabytes!

Obviously, you can do a lot in the file size area. BUT, look at what happened to the quality of color and the apparent sharpness. There are huge differences!

**Color:** All three JPEGs have radically changed the color. There's much more orange in the dove. Plus, the orange in the background of the image is much more intense (in design terms, the JPEGs have greatly increased the saturation of the color).

**Sharpness:** When comparing the image in the upper left to the one in the lower right, you can easily see that the max quality JPEG has radically increased the contrast—destroying much of the subtlety of both the bird and the background. The lower left version is quite a bit better. I suspect that a 60% quality will do even better. The upper right is simply unacceptable. It is no longer a professional grade image.

However, by resampling the PSD [Photoshop image] to 300 dpi at 5 inches wide and then saving as a 30% quality JPEG with no blurring [without using Save For Web], I get the image below. It retains the detail and controls the saturation [as seen between the dove's wings] while giving us a file size of 223 KB.

Now the only problem comes when I need to convert it to the resolution required for ePUB Reflows and MOBIs, which is 72 dpi and 600 pixels wide. This is going to deteriorate the image some more, as you can see below.

As you saw, the radically resampled image looks pretty good. It started as a free image from Pixabay at 3000 × 2236 pixels. It was resized and resampled in Photoshop from the original [saved as a PSD] to a 300 dpi, 1550x1118 JPEG for this booklet. Finally it was resized and resampled to 72 dpi, 600x447 pixel, 60% quality JPEG for use in reflowable ePUBs and MOBIs. The final ePUB version JPEG is even small enough [93 K] to be under the dangerous damage size of anything over 128 K in an Kindle book. More about that later.

## Using drawings & paintings

Paintings are done in Photoshop (or scanned and converted in Photoshop or GIMP), so they have the same resolution problems as we see above. For now, you'll just have to take my word for it about the quality of the 600 pixel wide ebook images. We'll talk about it more as we go forward.

**Scanned art:** this would include scanned pencil drawings, inkwork, or anything else. As soon as it is scanned the identical resolution and JPEG artifact issues arise.

The recommendation is to always scan at the highest resolution possible. I usually scan at 600 or 1200 dpi. Your scanner may not be able to do that. But you need to get a scanner that will work at 300 dpi, at least.

# Chapter 4

# The various file formats

We just spent some time dealing with some of the issues with JPEGs. This format has the most issues. You do need to be careful with JPEGs. However, there are several formats we use all the time. You need to be aware of all of them, and the special problems with each.

## Print image formats

### Raster

- **PSD:** this is the native Photoshop format. It is only accepted by InDesign, QuarkXPress, Illustrator, and Photoshop. These apps prefer PSDs. However, the self-publishing suppliers cannot handle vectors in PSDs.

- **TIFF:** This is raster only and required by Office for high resolution raster images. It supports layers, but they are only usable in InDesign, QuarkXPress, Illustrator, and Photoshop.

- **JPEG:** In general, this is only for ebooks. However, Photoshop will

Save As a high resolution JPEG. But, JPEGs are lossy and have artifacts.

### Vector plus Raster

- ❧ **PDF (Print Quality):** These can be all vector, a combination of both, or raster only (in the case of the Photoshop PDFs required by Createspace).

- ❧ **AI:** This is the native Illustrator Format. It can hold both vectors and raster images. It is only accepted by InDesign, QuarkXPress, Illustrator, and Photoshop.

- ❧ **EPS:** an old vector PostScript format which should be converted to PDF if possible.

## Ebook image formats

At this point, we are normally stuck with raster images. ePUBs and MOBI can accept SVG, which is vector. But only iBooks Author can actually handle SVG.

Plus, downloadable PDFs can handle any of the print formats well. The main thing to watch is file sizes. So use as many vector images as possible in PDF downloadable books.

- ❧ **JPEG:** Best for photos, unless you need transparency. 72 dpi images except for ePUB FXL [Fixed layout] which uses 150 dpi. Using Save For Web in Photoshop produces the best images. Use High, Very High, or Maximum quality (60% or higher) if possible to reduce artifacts. No transparency support. Powerful compression options, but they are lossy (you loose data in your images).

- ❧ **GIF:** 72 dpi, and very limited numbers of colors. Keep them at 256 colors, if possible. But for images with large areas of flat color, GIFs can become very small in file size. Transparency is supported and animation. Loss-less compression.

**PNG-24**: The 24 means millions of colors. 72 dpi. Very good for photos, but larger file sizes than JPEG. Supports partial transparency like smooth drop shadows and the like. It uses loss-less compression so your images are kept in better shape, though the file sizes may be larger. Very good for images with large flat areas of color.

**PNG-8**: Uses the same number of colors as a GIF, but the images are commonly better looking. Loss-less compression. Very good for images with large flat areas of color.

**BMP**: Usually only produced by Office products on Windows. They cannot be compressed so the file sizes are very large. Do not use them.

Most people, and I'm one of them, recommend using only JPEGs and PNGs. Again, using Photoshop's Save For Web dialog will give you the most control and the best images. But GIMP does well for ebook images also. These are the formats for your blog images also.

# Chapter 5

# Supplier Requirements

## Print Quality Images

First of all, for raster (also called bitmap) images, they must be 300 dpi. For the traditional printing suppliers, CMYK color is required. CMYK is the color of ink. RGB is the color of light. RGB has several things of which you need to be aware. For example, Red plus Green makes Yellow.

But it goes much further than that. There are several flavor of RGB. Printers like you to use Adobe RGB. PCs and the Web use sRGB. Adobe RGB is a much larger color space and can display many more colors than sRGB. But, you need software which can use it and a display or printer which can render it.

With Word, Scrivener, PowerPoint, and the like, sRGB is all they can handle. This does dull the color some. You need a Mac Desktop or Laptop to see them it is all irrelevant. Android machines and iOS machines are basically stuck with sRGB except the iPad Pro and the Galaxy 4 or better.

Most self-pub distributors cannot handle Adobe RGB either. They work in sRGB. Only Lightning Source, and individual on-demand printing companies can handle that level of color information. But they require conversion to CMYK. CMYK is severely limited when compared to RGB.

## Software Abilities

Only InDesign, Illustrator, Photoshop, and QuarkXPress can handle to image requirements of Lightning Source and traditional printing companies.

GIMP can only work in RGB. It supposedly can handle Adobe RGB, but only with difficulty.

## Image requirements for print

- **Lightning Source:** They require 300 dpi, CMYK

- **Blurb:** It has its own profiles for you to install in Photoshop and InDesign. They require 150-300 dpi, and sRGB.

- **Lulu:** They do not specify. So we can assume sRGB and 300 dpi.

- **Createspace:** They do not specify, but they will flag any images under 200 dpi—just a warning stating they will not be responsible for the blurriness of the images. They use sRGB.

- **Traditional printers and other on-demand printers:** They all want very specific image specifications. They will normally have a PDF or a Web page which tells you exactly what to do.

## Higher resolution does not help

In fact it will cause you problems. This is because submitting higher image resolutions than 300 dpi will cause their software to automatically downsample your images, and that will change them.

# Ebook images

As I mentioned, in general use JPEGs or PNGs at 72 dpi. Fixed layout ePUB FXL works better with 150 dpi images.

Downloadable PDFs, can use print quality images, but the file size can get very large. My training books, like *Book Production Using InDesign CC,* run 500 pages with over 300 images. The color PDFs get well over 20 MB. Even small booklets like this one will be over 2 MB, and I'm only using 14 images so far.

## Image requirements for the various versions

- **Downloadable PDFs:** Use print quality graphics as much as possible.

- **Kindle textbooks:** Use the print quality, color downloadable PDFs to produce a fixed layout Kindle book.

- **An ePUB FXL:** It uses JPEGs and PNGs at 150 dpi. These can be produced with Photoshop or GIMP, and probably Photoshop Elements. However, InDesign is the only application which makes ePUB FXL with any genuine ease.

- **An ePUB Reflowable:** 72 dpi, no more than 600 pixels wide or 800 pixels tall. JPEGs or PNGs.

- **Kindle Reflowable:** They accept GIF, JPEG, PNG, and BMP, but JPEGs and PNGs are best. They don't want anything taller than 500 pixels or wider than 600 pixels. Until recently, KDP required you to keep your images in your books under 128 KB. Supposedly that restriction is gone—maybe.

Larger images can be used in ePUBs and Kindle books (MOBI, .kf8, or the new .kfx) but you'll need to get into the code. Again iBooks Author is the only easy WYSIWYG ePUB producer for stuff like this. Supposedly InDesign can do it well also. But, I have not really tested that yet. With Word doc conversions, just watch very carefully for things untoward.

## Both ePUBs & blogs use HTML

In other words, images for your ePUBs & MOBI also work well for your blog postings and your social media marketing.

## Supplier support

- **The iBooks Store**: Reflowable ePUB2, ePUB3, and ePUB FXL

- **Kobo Writing Life**: Reflowable ePUB2, ePUB3, and ePUB FXL

- **Nookpress**: Reflowable ePUB2

- **Draft2Digital**: Unless you are letting them format your Word docs, they like Reflowable ePUBs: ePUB2 or ePUB3—but their marketing support is only for ePUB2

- **Smashwords**: Unless you are letting them meatgrind your Word docs, they like Reflowable ePUB2

- **Kindle KDP**: Use Kindle previewer to convert your ePUB Reflowable books—unless you are letting them format your Word docs.

- **Gumroad**: Downloadable PDF, ePUB Reflowable, and/or ePUB FXL books.

- **Others**: Check their requirements carefully.

## Acceptable software

Basically, it comes down to Photoshop and GIMP for ebook images. However, InDesign and Illustrator export good JPEGs and PNGs. I imagine the Corel apps do also.

In the PC world there are many options. But you need to be careful. Many of the lesser possibilities are really compromised in quality. If you are using freebie software, make sure the images are up to professional standards. Many of the cheap or free software just can't cut it.

*If you like this little booklet, please review it.*

# For book production training we offer:

This has a large section about Graphics in InDesign, plus everything else you need to self-publish professionally with the best software tools available.

It's available at all the normal online sites: Amazon, Barnes and Noble, the iBooks Store, Kobo, Gumroad, and my technical Website: *The Skilled Workman* at http://bergsland.org

*If you read it, please review it.*

# This is all part of Bergsland Design

At this point, all my work is done online. You'll find it at my website/blog which is called *The Skilled Workman*. I've been working online since 1996. I now am there exclusively under the Bergsland Design name, or the name of my Christian publishing house, Radiqx Press.

Radiqx Press has its own Website/blog, *Reality Calling*. It specializes in book reviews and support for Christian authors of speculative fiction. We now have four full-time reviewers, two of which specialize in redemptive romances.

Visit the sites, please

## The Skilled Workman

http://bergsland.org

## Radiqx Press/Reality Calling

http://radiqx.com

Or you are welcome to email me directly:

david@radiqx.com

*Thanks for reading this book!*

David

MANKATO, MINNESOTA AUGUST 2016

www.ingramcontent.com/pod-product-compliance
Lightning Source LLC
Chambersburg PA
CBHW050841180526

45159CB00004B/1986

www.ingramcontent.com/pod-product-compliance
Lightning Source LLC
Chambersburg PA
CBHW050841180526
45159CB00004B/1986